G000161061

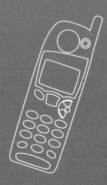

YOU KNOW YOU'RE A CHILD OF THE 1990s WHEN...

CHARLIE ELLIS

summersdale

YOU KNOW YOU'RE A CHILD OF THE 1990s WHEN...

This revised and updated edition copyright © Summersdale Publishers Ltd, 2020
First published in 2016

Text by Lucy York

Illustrations by Rita Kovács and Julie Goldsmith; icons © Shutterstock.com

An Hachette UK Company
www.hachette.co.uk

Summersdale Publishers Ltd
Part of Octopus Publishing Group Limited
Carmelite House
50 Victoria Embankment
LONDON
EC4Y 0DZ
UK

www.summersdale.com

Printed and bound in China

ISBN: 978-1-78783-345-6

Substantial discounts on bulk quantities of Summersdale books are available to corporations, professional associations, and other organizations. For details contact general enquiries: telephone: +44 (0) 1243 771107 email: enquiries@summersdale.com.

To...

From...

YOU KNOW YOU'RE A CHILD OF THE 1990s WHEN...

You still talk about **"videos,"** even though you only have digital subscription services now.

You used to wear **stick-on earrings** and **transfer tattoos**.

You never could get to grips with those **Magic Eye** pictures but you never let on.

You thought **Hypercolor T-shirts** were the best thing ever invented.

Beanie Babies

You still have a box of these somewhere in your parents' garage (tags on, of course). These adorably squidgy bean-filled creatures that each came with a unique name tag and poem were THE ultimate 1990s collectible. Though the Beanie bubble has long since burst, if you have a Patti the Platypus or Peanut the Royal Blue Elephant, it could still be worth a lot.

Furbies

For children, a super-cute furry friend that would talk and play games with you; for adults, the most annoying toy ever invented. This fountain of semi-comprehensible baby talk and painfully audible mechanics was the curse of many households and also responsible for many a battery drought—usually when you had almost taught your Furby to sing.

GAME BOYS

The ultimate status symbol, we begged, pleaded, and even did extra chores to get a Game Boy. Although today's video-game graphics are increasingly "realistic," we could hold entire worlds in our hands, and experience epic adventures out of just a few little black pixels and a gravelly, but endlessly inventive, 4-bit soundtrack. It also gave your lungs a workout, when the game cartridge needed blowing clean.

YOU KNOW YOU'RE A CHILD OF THE 1990s WHEN...

You feel intensely grateful that Facebook and cellphones with video-recording capabilities didn't exist while you were **learning how to party.**

You used to **call** your friends at **home**, one by one, to arrange a time and a place for meeting them—and you actually turned up at that place and time.

You got all your CD singles from **Sam Goody** or **The Wall**.

Your idea of dancing was lurching about in a **long jumper** while looking longingly at the floor.

1. Which educational TV show featured a cartoon butterfly in the opening sequence?

2. What type of animal was Ren, of *The Ren & Stimpy Show* fame?

3. What was the name of the spiky-haired, big bead-wearing rollerblader in *Heartbreak High*?

4. What type of animal was Arthur's best friend, Buster?

5 What were the names of the twins from *Rugrats*?

6 Helga Pataki was a character on which show?

7 What was the name of Tim's neighbor (whose full face was rarely seen) in *Home Improvement*?

8 What song does Barney sing at the end of every episode of *Barney & Friends*?

Answers: 1. *Reading Rainbow* **2.** Chihuahua
3. (Alan) Bolton **4.** Rabbit **5.** Phil and Lil **6.** *Hey Arnold!*
7. Wilson **8.** "I Love You"

11

YOU KNOW YOU'RE A CHILD OF THE 1990s WHEN...

You can get a guaranteed laugh from your friends by saying **"Yada, yada, yada"** or announcing **"No soup for you!"**

You still secretly believe that
"the truth is out there."

Forget spiders; the
creepy-crawly you most feared
was the **Millennium Bug**.

You were impressed by Ally
McBeal—not by her high-flying
career but because of her
enormous pout.

Boy Meets World

This coming-of-age series followed best friends Cory and Shawn as they navigated the tricky waters of adolescence. It taught us some important lessons and brought us one of the most memorable onscreen teen romances of all time.

Dinosaurs

Thanks to this wacky sitcom featuring just your average family of dinosaurs, playgrounds around the country echoed with cries of "Gotta love me!," "AGAIN!" and "Not the momma!"

Mighty Morphin Power Rangers

Everyone had a favorite among this multi-colored band of teens with attitude. Who else could do battle with giant, dino-shaped robots while wearing skin tight all-in-ones?

3rd Rock from the Sun

This kooky family of aliens weren't always so good at mastering the art of human behavior. Still, with plenty of puns around Dick Soloman's name and a guest appearance from "supreme leader" William Shatner, you can see why everyone still loves this show.

Sabrina the Teenage Witch

Admit it, you secretly hoped that your sixteenth birthday would bring you magical witch powers, or failing that, at least a talking cat. Lovable, loopy Sabrina had many a magical mishap and we couldn't help but love her for it.

Bill Nye the Science Guy

Every episode was a half-hour of nerdy fast-paced fun with this Way Cool Scientist. With his bowtie firmly tied and dad jokes at the ready, Bill Nye brought science to life through his Nifty Home Experiments, Clever Science Tricks, and Soundtrack of Science.

YOU KNOW YOU'RE A CHILD OF THE 1990s WHEN...

You were curious about how shocking the interview scene in *Basic Instinct* really was.

You were elated—and endlessly frustrated—with a little game called **Screwball Scramble**.

Any knowledge you have of the literary classics is all thanks to **Wishbone,** the Jack Russell terrier.

You spent all of your money in the arcade—on games like *The Simpsons* and *After Burner* —before you even got near the movie theater.

QUIZ

ONLY A CHILD OF THE 1990s WILL KNOW...

1. Which one-handed Yankee player famously threw a no-hitter against the Cleveland Indians in 1993?

2. Which former NFL champion was behind the wheel of the most-watched car chase of all time in 1994?

3. Which part of Evander Holyfield's body did Mike Tyson famously bite?

5. At the 1992 Barcelona Olympics, which athlete won the men's 100m gold medal?

4. Which Olympic figure skater was struck on the knee with a police baton in 1994 in a bid to prevent her competing in future championships?

6. Which Buffalo Bills player famously missed a 47-yard field goal at the Super Bowl XXV in 1991, prompting the commentator to say "No good… wide right!"?

7. At the 1996 Atlanta Olympics, what injury meant that gymnast Kerri Strug had to be carried to the podium to collect her gold medal?

8. What was Jean Van de Velde's score on the last hole at the 1999 Open Championship, after his famous "collapse"?

Answers: 1. Jim Abbott **2.** O.J. Simpson **3.** His ear **4.** Linford Christie **5.** Nancy Kerrigan **6.** Scott Norwood **7.** A broken ankle **8.** Triple-bogey seven

YOU KNOW YOU'RE A CHILD OF THE 1990s WHEN...

After watching **Four Weddings and a Funeral** when it first came out, you thought all men would be like Hugh Grant—until you started dating.

You always wanted to be Mr. Black among your buddies, but somehow you always ended up as **Mr. Pink**.

You can remember being told off by your parents for saying **"Eat my shorts!"** to your grandma.

All movie nights began with a trip to **Blockbuster**.

The Simpsons

Who can forget this all-encompassing craze of the 1990s? Matt Groening and Co. made TV history with a show that was as fun for adults as it was for kids. Cue the waves of Simpsons merchandise, which included a cassette album entitled *The Simpsons Sing the Blues*, featuring the groovy epic "Do the Bartman."

Friends

Which "Friend" were you? We got entirely the wrong idea about what it was like to be young and living in New York City, but we loved it anyway. It was pretty much the first box set everyone got and, with ten seasons, there was plenty to be had.

THE FRESH PRINCE OF BEL-AIR

All 1990s children know that the coolest Will Smith character is the Fresh Prince. He had the quickest lines, the most laid-back attitude, and the most outrageous clothes. Throw in a brilliant supporting cast—including the ever-goofy Carlton and the dim-witted Jazz—and you have a hit. Here's betting you can rap along to the theme tune!

YOU KNOW YOU'RE A CHILD OF THE 1990s WHEN...

You quizzed the careers officer at school about the qualifications required to be a pet detective after watching **Ace Ventura**.

No trip to the mall was complete without stopping by **Limited Too**, the **Warner Bros. Studio Store**, and **Suncoast Motion Picture Co**.

You went crazy for gross-out toys involving **slime**, gak, and **goo**.

You can remember being proud to wear your free **neon** (pink, green, or yellow) McDonald's shades that came with your **Happy Meal**.

ONLY A CHILD OF THE 1990s WILL KNOW...

1 With what toy could you "walk the dog" and "rock the cradle"?

2 What rival brand (free in your bag of chips) competed with Pogs for playground popularity?

3 What did the color black generally indicate on a mood ring?

4 What was the last piece to be built in the game Mousetrap?

5 What four-letter word is called out when two people say the same word at the same time?

6 What was the name of the original lobster Beanie Baby?

7 What was the name of the elasticated, shirtless doll that also had a bendable canine pal?

8 What was the name of the frustrating audio game that commanded you to "twist it" and "pull it"?

YOU KNOW YOU'RE A CHILD OF THE 1990s WHEN...

You can remember begging your parents for a pair of **Spice Girls**-style chunky-heeled shoes or **Reebok Pumps**. But instead you got something out of the local thrift store.

From your lunchbox to your pencil case, from folders to erasers, all your school supplies had to be **Lisa Frank**.

You still check under the bed for **Gremlins** before going to sleep.

You still have a thing for **Pierce Brosnan**—even though you have to admit that his Bond was below par.

DO YOU REMEMBER...

Titanic

Oh come on, you know you cried while watching *Titanic*. It starts out with heart-throb of the decade Leo being cool and having epic curtains—and then BAM! You're sobbing your heart out with a frosty Kate Winslet. There was totally still room on that raft...

Jurassic Park

Nothing could prepare us for the terrifying, the thrilling, the dino-riffic *Jurassic Park*. We'd never seen anything like it, and we were pretty sure that the dinosaurs were real 'cause there's no way you could fake animals that looked that genuine.

Terminator 2: Judgment Day

Wait—what? The baddie is now... a goodie? Spoilers if you haven't seen *Terminator 2* yet but c'mon! If you haven't then you've deprived yourself of one of the coolest movies ever!

The Lion King

Some people like to waffle about how the movie is based on *Hamlet* but, frankly, who cares? There are singing lions, singing hyenas, and singing and farting warthogs. The 1990s was a classic era for blockbusting Disney movies—and this is arguably the best.

Four Weddings and a Funeral

At the time, it wasn't clear what this movie was about. You only knew two things about it: your mom would watch it on VHS and cry—but it was still her favorite movie—and it was one of the umpteen-billion movies featuring Hugh Grant and his floppy hair.

Home Alone

For several blissful days, Kevin McCallister lived the life we dreamed about (except for the part about being terrorized by burglars): eating whatever he wanted, watching whatever he wanted, no one to boss him around... and we may have tried to make an ill-advised booby trap or two ourselves.

YOU KNOW YOU'RE A CHILD OF THE 1990s WHEN...

You desperately wanted to pass your driving test so that you and your buddies could re-enact the "Bohemian Rhapsody" head-banging scene in *Wayne's World*.

You still can't believe your friends made you ask for *Fight Club* soap at the drugstore.

You tried every DIY make in *Room by Room*.

When you first made an email account, even the **delivery failed**.

QUIZ

1. The fictional town of Stoneybrook, Connecticut, was the setting for which popular book series?

2. Which 1990s classic opens with "On a dark, dark hill there was a dark, dark town"?

3. Name at least two of the original Animorphs.

4. What was the name of Jessica Wakefield's twin sister in the *Sweet Valley High* series?

5 What was the name of the teacher who took her pupils on field trips to impossible locations in *The Magic School Bus* series?

6 How many strawberries does the very hungry caterpillar eat?

7 With what vehicle did Harry and Ron arrive at Hogwarts at the start of *Harry Potter and the Chamber of Secrets*?

8 Complete this book title: *Amber Brown is Not a* _____

YOU KNOW YOU'RE A CHILD OF THE 1990s WHEN...

You can't think of a single Shakespeare play without an image of **Kenneth Branagh** popping into your head.

The first thing you think of when you hear the names Britney Spears, Justin Timberlake, Christina Aguilera, and Ryan Gosling is *The All-New Mickey Mouse Club*.

You remember when **Doritos** were **3D**.

You wouldn't consider going out without squirting yourself all over with **CK One**.

Scrunchies

If your scrunchie wasn't bigger than your head, then you just weren't cool. Not really, but it was true that the bigger the scrunchie, the better. A scrunchie matched to your top was a fashion must.

Choker Necklaces

Any choker was great but the best of all were those "tattoo" stretch ones. You could get them at any good Claire's Accessories or even at the dollar-store. Paired with a handful of other pendant necklaces to look your best.

JELLY
SANDALS

What's better than jelly sandals? Glitter jelly
sandals! Uncomfortable, strappy, and a bit
sticky, the jelly sandal was nonetheless
the most beloved item in our wardrobes.
Wearing those made you feel like a
modern, funky princess.

YOU KNOW YOU'RE A CHILD OF THE 1990s WHEN...

You remember what you were doing the moment you heard **Kurt Cobain** had died.

You only agreed to go on a **date** with the boy next door because he had tickets to see **Pearl Jam**.

You once owned a whole set of **neon-colored socks**.

On a sunny day, the **reflective glare** from your frosted or glossed lips was enough to cause temporary blindness.

QUIZ

ONLY A CHILD OF THE 1990s WILL KNOW...

1. What was the name of the tiny candy that came in a box of two halves?

2. Which cereal, launched in 1995, resembled tiny pieces of dried bread?

3. Which lunchbox craze contained mini crackers, meats, and cheeses, and came with a Capri Sun on the side?

4 On which candy could you "play real music"?

5 Finish this famous food commercial catchphrase: "I feel like _ tonight."

6 What was the name of the unusual "clear cola" that appeared in shops in the early 1990s?

7 What were the two initial variations of Sunny D, named after US states?

8 What two sweet foodstuffs were combined in Dunk-a-roos?

YOU KNOW YOU'RE A CHILD OF THE 1990s WHEN...

You remember the **pain** of having to wait until your video (or album cassette) **rewound**. It felt like an eternity!

You went around to a friend's house mostly because they had a **SodaStream**.

You have fond memories of singing: "**Gillette**, the best a man can get!" to your brother after he incurred his first shaving injury.

You spent hours coming up with inventive ways to eat a **Reese's Peanut Butter Cup,** because there is no wrong way.

DO YOU REMEMBER...

Crew-Neck Sweaters

These sweaters weren't for wearing; they were for tying around your waist. And also for inevitably getting caught in the chain when you tried to cycle with them on.

Baseball Caps

It's said that scientists have studied for years to discover the exact coolest angle to wear a baseball cap. They're still not sure but it seems to be at any angle but facing the front.

Turtlenecks

Now we think of it, it's not clear why the sweater beloved of librarians and embarrassing dads everywhere was so in, but it was. And we have the photos, sadly, to prove it.

Puka Shell Necklaces

We may not have ever seen a surfboard in our lives, let alone Hawaii, but puka shell necklaces were a must-have item. Strangely, jewelry for dudes hasn't really been in fashion since. Wonder why...

Baggy

So "baggy" isn't really an item of clothing or jewelry, but for us 1990s kids, it was a way of life. Whether you were grunge or loved rap, the name of the game was baggy jeans, topped by a baggy tee, topped by a baggy shirt, topped by a baggy sweatshirt.

YOU KNOW YOU'RE
A CHILD OF THE
1990s
WHEN...

You remember nursing your ankle for hours after a **Skip It** misstep.

You remember the first time you saw *The Jerry Springer Show*— and it blew your mind!

You borrowed your dad's **Handycam** to make your own version of *The Blair Witch Project*.

You may not have been born with great legs, but thanks to the **Thighmaster** you could look like you were.

QUIZ

ONLY A CHILD OF
THE 1990s WILL KNOW...

1. Which of these were NOT a 1990s celebrity couple?
   A. Brad and Angelina
   B. Johnny and Winona
   C. Britney and Justin

2. Who was the highest-paid actor in Hollywood in 1995? (Clue: he starred in *Judge Dredd* in that year.)

3. Frances Bean Cobain was born in which year?

4 The music video for which Aerosmith hit featured a young Alicia Silverstone jumping from an overpass?

5 Liz Hurley wore a black dress famously held together by what?

6 Which couple famously featured in the first ever leaked celebrity sex tape in 1995?

7 Madonna's iconic cone bra was designed by which fashion designer?

8 Orange soda was the favorite drink of which kids' sitcom character?

YOU KNOW YOU'RE A CHILD OF THE 1990s WHEN...

Whenever you needed to find
something out, you would
just **Ask Jeeves.**

You remember **Harry Potter** best as a character in a book—not as a child movie star.

You always get the irresistible urge to re-enact the iconic prow scene in *Titanic* whenever you find yourself on a **ferry**.

You still believe, in all honesty, that you are **Bridget Jones** (or Mark Darcy).

Curtains

Sigh. This floppy, gelled 'do was the province of heart-throbs everywhere, from Brad Pitt to Leonardo DiCaprio. The only way for a hairstyle to be more 1990s was if you added highlights.

Tiny Buns

With one of the decade's more... original styles, girls everywhere wondered: why have one bun on your head when you could have a dozen? Fixed in place with miniscule, painful rubber bands, the effect was "knobbly" to say the least.

THE RACHEL

No list of 1990s hairstyles can go without mention of The Rachel. Highlights, layers, *Friends*; it was like someone took the decade and made it into a haircut. To our disappointment, getting The Rachel didn't make us look like Jennifer Aniston, though.

YOU KNOW YOU'RE A CHILD OF THE 1990s WHEN...

You'll always prefer the **Hanson** brothers to the Jonas Brothers.

You indulged in the see-through, colored plastic pacifier craze while at school.

You thought having a **pager** was the height of modern technological advancement.

Mario Kart, Street Fighter II, and *Doom* were (and still are) at the top of your **Super Nintendo** video game favorites list.

QUIZ

ONLY A CHILD OF THE 1990s WILL KNOW...

1. What was the highest-selling video game of the 1990s? (Clue: it was for Game Boy.)

2. Which gadget released in 1998 delivered email messages straight to your wrist?

3. What species is Mario's nemesis Bowser?

4. The DualShock controller enhanced gameplay in what way?

5 What technological innovation made running, or even walking, with Discmans much easier?

6 Before cellphones were widespread, what text-only gadget was used for high-speed communication in the 1990s?

7 Which Apple product, famous for its jazzy casing, brought the company back into profitability?

8 The Dreamcast console, now defunct, was released by which company in 1998?

YOU KNOW YOU'RE A CHILD OF THE 1990s WHEN...

You begged your parents to buy you the new—bigger, badder—**Super Soaker** after seeing the commercial on TV.

Bill and Ted, Beavis and Butt-Head, and Thelma and Louise are some of your on-screen heroes.

'You have fond memories of the phrases "How you doin?" and "She's your lobster."

You had heated debates about whether Airwalk sneakers were better than Vans.

DO YOU REMEMBER...

"Wannabe"

It didn't matter what music you were into, by the end of 1996 you knew all the words to this song. Kicking off the brief world-domination of the Spice Girls and "girl power," kids everywhere blasted this from their tape players.

"Un-Break My Heart"

This ultimate tearjerker warbled its way to the top of the charts in 1996 and stayed there for 11 weeks. The music video featured lots of flashbacks to Toni Braxton and her model lover frolicking about in black silk pajamas, and an opening scene that demonstrated how *not* to remove a motorbike accident victim's helmet.

"Smells Like Teen Spirit"

Either someone took all your angst and made it into a perfect song or you were listening to a wall of senseless noise; Nirvana's "Teen Spirit" wasn't for everyone, but for those who appreciated it, it was the start of a love affair with grunge.

"End of the Road"

Boyz II Men had us all crooning "I belong to youuuuu!" back in 1992, but hopefully by now the boys have accepted the break up and moved on.

"... Baby One More Time"

Strangely sad lyrics? Check. Inappropriate schoolgirl uniform? Big check. And yet somehow this was a pop smash hit, transforming Britney Spears into a super-megastar!

YOU KNOW YOU'RE A CHILD OF THE 1990s WHEN...

You remember **Arnold Schwarzenegger** better as the Terminator rather than the Governator.

You indicated that things were all cool with a casual **"Cowabunga, dude."**

You lived for the day when the gym teacher got the **rainbow parachute** out.

Even now, you still can't get your **Tamagotchi** to survive longer than two weeks.

QUIZ

ONLY A CHILD OF THE 1990s WILL KNOW...

1. In the lamentable 1993 movie *Super Mario Bros.*, Mario is played by which actor?

2. In *Jurassic Park*, the velociraptors are defeated by which dinosaur?

3. Who wrote the soundtrack for the 1992 Disney smash hit, *The Lion King*?

4. Which famous showstopping song do the Gremlins, in *Gremlins 2: The New Batch*, sing near the end of the movie?

5 What was the model number of the terminator chasing John Connor in *Terminator 2*?

6 *Clueless* was an updated movie version of which classic novel? (Clue: it's by Jane Austen.)

7 What color pill did Neo take in order to "wake up" to reality?

8 In the *Austin Powers* sequel, *The Spy Who Shagged Me*, what precious item did Austin lose?

Answers 1. Bob Hoskins **2.** T-Rex
3. Tim Rice and Elton John **4.** "New York, New York"
5. T-1000 **6.** Emma **7.** Red **8.** His mojo

YOU KNOW YOU'RE A CHILD OF THE 1990s WHEN...

You know what **Pogs** and **Tazos** are, but never quite figured out how to use them.

You know how to
"party like it's **1999**."

90210 just doesn't sound
the same without Beverly
Hills in front of it.

You were shocked to discover
that *Northern Exposure*
wasn't shot in Alaska.

"Whassup?"

Whhaaaaaassssuuuuuuuup? No further discussion needed.

"Take a chill pill"

When parents, teachers, and friends alike were all going postal and you weren't having it, telling them to take a chill pill was the obvious solution. Surprisingly, the advice rarely helped people to calm down.

"Talk to the hand"

'Cause the face ain't listenin'. This ultimate dismissal for when you just didn't want to hear what somebody had to say was accompanied by a palm thrust rudely in the speaker's direction.

"... NOT!"

To be said loudly and with great defiance at the end of a sentence that you didn't mean, this was our first foray into the usually more subtle world of sarcasm. Also, one of the many 1990s catchphrases popularized by hard-rockin' duo Wayne and Garth (Mike Myers and Dana Carvey) of *Saturday Night Live*, *Wayne's World* and *Wayne's World 2* fame. Party on!

YOU KNOW YOU'RE A CHILD OF THE 1990s WHEN...

A moustache didn't look good on anyone—except your dad, **Ned Flanders**, and Hulk Hogan.

You didn't see anything wrong with spending your Friday night watching *Perfect Strangers, Full House,* and *Family Matters.*

You remember when **Madonna** and **Vanilla Ice** were an item.

Your bedroom ceiling was covered in **glow-in-the-dark** stars.

QUIZ

ONLY A CHILD OF THE 1990s WILL KNOW...

1. The construction of which habitable satellite began in 1995?

2. Which popular online auction site was founded in 1995?

3. Which famous singer died of an HIV-related illness in 1991?

4. What was the name of the world's first successfully cloned mammal?

5 Where did the Pathfinder land on July 4, 1997?

6 In 1994, which sport did basketball god Michael Jordan switch to?

7 The World Wide Web was made public in what year?

8 What was the name of the intern that President Bill Clinton "did not" have sexual relations with?

Answers: 1. The International Space Station **2.** eBay
3. Freddie Mercury **4.** Dolly the Sheep **5.** On Mars
6. Minor league baseball (Chicago White Sox) **7.** 1991
8. Monica Lewinsky

75

YOU KNOW YOU'RE A CHILD OF THE 1990s WHEN...

You have fond memories of reading *Teen People* and *Seventeen*.

Every time you visit a swamp you listen out for the call of the elusive **Budweiser frog**.

You logically thought: the **bigger** the speakers, the **louder** the music.

Whenever you meet a British person you have the strong urge to tell them to **"Behave"** and to shout **"Yeah baby!"**

Dial-up

Sometimes, when it's quiet, we can still hear the screeching of a dial-up modem ringing in our ears. Oh the days when you would try to sneak as much time on the internet as possible, while your parents shouted for you to get off because they wanted to use the phone.

The Millennium Bug

It was pretty much the coming of the apocalypse: the millennium bug was going to shut down everything electronic and completely wipe out the internet—and we wouldn't even be able to go on AOL. The end was truly near.

NOKIA 5110

In the late 1990s, cellphones were IT—and, as with everything else, it mattered what brand of phone you had! Never mind having the internet or a camera on there, it was quite enough having a personalized monophonic ringtone and *Snake*.

YOU KNOW YOU'RE
A CHILD OF THE
1990s
WHEN...

You think the sound of monks singing doesn't quite work unless there's an electronic beat in the background.

You can't get "I'll be back"
out of your vocabulary.

Sunday nights will always be the
best time to settle down and
watch *The Wonderful
World of Disney*.

You might have known all the lyrics
to "Baby Got Back," but looking
back you seriously question why
your parents let you listen to it.

QUIZ

1. Which Carter was a member of the Backstreet Boys?
   A. Nick Carter
   B. Aaron Carter
   C. John Carter

2. What was Kris Kross going to make you do?

3. Which member of TLC burned her boyfriend's house down?

4 Which song by Shaggy was featured on a Levi's commercial?

5 Whitney Houston stayed at the top of the Billboard Hot 100 with "I Will Always Love You" for how many weeks?

6 Which controversial Prodigy video won Best Dance Video and Breakthrough Video at the 1998 MTV Video Music Awards?

7 What species was the pitiful main character in Daft Punk's "Da Funk" video?

8 Madonna released a coffee table book in 1992 entitled what?

YOU KNOW YOU'RE A CHILD OF THE 1990s WHEN...

You aspired to be like—at least—one of the characters in *Saved by the Bell* (except maybe Screech!).

You're still wondering where in the world **Carmen Sandiego** is.

You have a pair of **Hammer pants** lurking in your closet—because they were "too legit to quit."

You couldn't decide whether your biggest tennis crush was **Agassi** or **Sampras**.

Sony Walkman/Discman

The 1990s were a time of great revolution in portable music! By the end of the decade, we had made the shift from cassette tapes to shiny CDs, buying fancy cases to house our extensive collections.

Super Nintendo

Nintendo had already proven they were the kings of video game consoles, with the legendary NES. Like everything in the 1990s, sticking "super" in front of a name was all it took to make it sound like the best thing ever. The Super Nintendo might have been just that.

PlayStation

Crash Bandicoot, Spyro the Dragon, Lara Croft, Abe, Rayman—for years these were our good buddies, transporting us to new worlds. Although, with the highs came the lows: remember the pain of scratching a disk or trying to decide which game to delete off your memory card to make room for your new save?

Floppy Disks

Remember all those movies where the hero needed to steal some world-saving information and it was all on a super high-tech floppy disk? Remember when one of those high-tech floppy disks would get stuck in your computer and you had to raid the cutlery drawer to get it out? We never saw that in the movies!

Sega Mega Drive

Sonic the Hedgehog, Streets of Rage, Micro Machines... the 1990s really were the glory days of gaming. The only downside was falling out with our Super Nintendo-owning friends over which console was better.

Easy-Bake Oven

Doing chores sucked but having an Easy-Bake Oven was the coolest! A dusty ancestor of the meal-in-a-mug trend, all you had to do was press a button and you'd made some cake—or at least that's what it seemed like. If only we were as keen on cooking now.

You remember telling your friends that *The Lord of the Rings* was too huge and epic to ever appear as a movie (especially having seen the disjointed 1978 attempt!).

You owned a **zebra-print**
slap bracelet.

Your wardrobe was incomplete
unless it included a pair of
Bongo Jeans.

Just thinking about the opening
theme from *Unsolved Mysteries*
sends a chill down your spine.

QUIZ

ONLY A CHILD OF THE 1990s WILL KNOW...

1 Which girly, flight-capable toy was recalled in 2000 after causing more than 100 injuries since its 1994 release?

2 In the board game Gooey Louie, what was the main method of play?

3 What miniscule hero was sold with playsets named "Doom Zones" and "Horror Heads"?

4 What color was the electronic voice-recorder Dear Diary?

5 What toy's appeal lay in your ability to draw on it, only to wash it all off and start again?

6 What was the name of the chunky, spring-loaded shoes loved by kids the world over?

7 Which life-sized doll released in 1992 allowed owners to wear and share her outfits?

8 In which popular board game did players have to sneak into the kitchen for a snack?

YOU KNOW YOU'RE A CHILD OF THE 1990s WHEN...

The real reason you bought an **Aerobie Flying Ring** was so that you could pretend you were Xena: Warrior Princess.

You're glad that giant headphones are cool again— you can get your old ones out of the attic!

Rollerblades (and to some extent "quads") were the most street-credible mode of transport.

The "Macarena" was played at least twice at your prom.

DO YOU REMEMBER...

Kate Moss

Was there anything more 1990s than Kate Moss modeling for Calvin Klein? Fresh-faced and waifish, she was the complete opposite of the tall and curvy supermodels of the day, such as Cindy Crawford and Naomi Campbell.

Jonathan Taylor Thomas

The cutest sibling on *Home Improvement* and the voice of Simba in *The Lion King*, J.T.T. was all anyone wanted to talk about on school lunchbreak and the odds were there was a poster of him hanging on the wall of at least one bedroom in every home.

BEAVIS AND BUTT-HEAD

Who would have thought that two morally impaired, moronic teenagers whose sole goals in life were to eat as much junk food as possible, watch TV, and score with girls would have captivated millions of TV viewers? And yet Beavis and Butt-head did just that, taking sniggering at sexual innuendos to a whole new level.

NACHOS RULE!!!

YOU KNOW YOU'RE A CHILD OF THE 1990s WHEN...

You developed frostbite in your midriff because of your insistence on wearing **crop tops** in any weather—or got injured from wearing holographic "Lennon" **sunglasses** at night.

You had a massive crush on **Aladdin** and / or **Jasmine**.

You still can't get over how Batman movies went from gothic (*Batman*, ***Batman Returns***) to goofy (*Batman Forever*, ***Batman and Robin***). George Clooney— what were they thinking?!

You tried to tell your parents that you **wouldn't get out of bed** for less than 10,000 sweets a day.

QUIZ

ONLY A CHILD OF THE 1990s WILL KNOW...

1 Which early nineties cult TV show centered around the investigation of the murder of Laura Palmer?

2 In which city did brothers Frasier and Niles Crane live?

3 Who played Brenda Walsh in the hit teen soap opera *Beverly Hills 90210*?

4 What was the catchphrase of lead character Dr. Sam Beckett in *Quantum Leap*?

5 Which Warner Bros. series featured cartoon creatures that were "zany to the max"?

6 What was the name of Marshall's best friend and sidekick in *Eerie, Indiana*?

7 In which NBC sitcom did Mayim Bialik play a precocious teenage girl with a fondness for floppy hats?

8 *The New Adventures of Superman* featured which actor in the lead role of Clark Kent / Superman?

Answers: 1. *Twin Peaks* **2.** Seattle **3.** Shannen Doherty **4.** "Oh boy!" **5.** *Animaniacs* **6.** Simon **7.** *Blossom* **8.** Dean Cain

YOU KNOW YOU'RE A CHILD OF THE 1990s WHEN...

You spent the last half of 1999 doing *Matrix* slo-mo bends in the playground.

You owned weekend sneakers, **everyday sneakers**, and "formal" sneakers.

You knew all the words to **"Ironic,"** even if you didn't exactly know what "ironic" meant.

You pretty much melted your tongue off with a **Warhead** sour sweet.

Nestlé Magic Balls

These chocolate balls in foil in a box had us all wondering what surprise we would find inside. Invariably it was a collectible plastic Disney figurine, until the fun police put an end to that in 1997, branding them a choking hazard. They made a comeback as Wonder Balls in 2000, with candy inside instead of plastic toys, but it was never quite the same.

Bagel Bites

The perfect snack for pizza lovers: because when your pizza comes on a bagel, you can eat it anytime! Kids went wild for these in the 90s and their popularity has endured to this day, even inspiring Meat Loaf to famously sing about them on *Late Night with Jimmy Fallon*.

BABY BOTTLE POPS

We're not really sure why an undersized baby's bottle full of sherbet was so popular, but it was something to do with the cheesy and immensely catchy commercial, which reliably informed us we could lick it, shake it, and drink it. The novelty factor was the main draw, as was the case with similar sweets like Push Pops and Chupa Chups with bubblegum inside.

YOU KNOW YOU'RE A CHILD OF THE 1990s WHEN...

You learned all you needed to know about what Michael Jordan did between his retirement from NBA in 1993 and his comeback in 1995 from *Space Jam*.

You can remember a time
when a can of **soda** was less
than **50 cents.**

No back-to-school survival pack
was complete without a **Trapper
Keeper** and a collection of
Troll pencil-toppers.

You sort of looked like a bug, with
your scraped-back **ponytail** and
two strands of hair coming
down your face.

QUIZ

1. The dubious combination of a skirt and shorts was known as what?

2. Naomi Campbell took a tumble on the runway modeling for which designer? (Clue: V.W.)

3. If you crossed a belt and an oversized wallet, what would you get?

4. What kind of hairdressing implement has a spirit level?

5 What was the name for the waifish, gaunt style of high fashion?

6 What type of childish dress was beloved of the riot grrrl and grunge movements?

7 What body piercing came to popularity after Christy Turlington showed hers off in 1993?

8 What was the name of the leggings with straps that slipped under the heel?

Answers: 1. A skort **2.** Vivienne Westwood **3.** A fanny pack
4. A flat-topper **5.** Heroin chic **6.** Babydoll
7. Belly-button piercing **8.** Stirrup leggings

107

YOU KNOW YOU'RE A CHILD OF THE 1990s WHEN...

You bore witness to the unholy union of two of the decade's most popular **music** genres: rap and metal. And so it was that **"Nu Metal"** was created.

You remember a time when the only music you could buy on vinyl was for **dance music** DJs.

At least half your pocket money was spent on **hair gel**.

You were never worried about where your wallet was because it was in your pocket, attached by your trusty **wallet chain**.

DO YOU REMEMBER...

Troll Dolls

The beauty of Troll Dolls was that there were just so many. Big ones, small ones, pencil toppers, backpacks—they were everywhere. Our rooms looked like some sort of sci-fi nightmare.

Talkboy

After watching *Home Alone 2: Lost in New York*, you begged your parents for one of these cassette player/recorders so that you could fool grown-ups into thinking you were an adult on the phone, just like Kevin McCallister.

Pokémon Cards

The purists will argue that the cards were a mere commercialization of the games, but who cared—there were "shinies" to be found and trades to be made. Very little actual gameplay went on; it was far more satisfying to sit and compare whose deck was better than whose.

Tickle Me Elmo

Your parents would have risked life and limb to secure you one of these coveted toys in the infamous shopping frenzy of 1996, when the Elmo craze was at its peak. Given that all the toy did was vibrate and giggle, you now wonder what all the fuss was about.

Skateboards

Remember: Those who can't, fingerskate. And actually, apart from the blessed few, those who couldn't still tried to skate. We may have just about been able to mount the curb but we had dreams of massive half-pipes and being christened "the new Tony Hawk".

Backpacks

Tiny backpacks, smiley-face backpacks, furry backpacks, animal backpacks—there was seemingly no end to how cool they were. And if your backpack wasn't cool, you could tag it so it looked awesome (to the annoyance of the parent who had just bought it!).

YOU KNOW YOU'RE
A CHILD OF THE
1990s
WHEN...

You thought anything could be
made out of just a few sheets
of tissue paper and three-parts
water, one-part **school glue**.

You owned a pair of **snap-fastened** sweatpants.

Your **favorite** bands were all a strange mix of letters and numbers: **98°, Blink 182**, 3T...

Your parents had to cut out at least one **twisty hair gem** from your hair.

QUIZ

1. Skechers put themselves on the map with a sneaker named what? (Clue: Round, shiny metal.)

2. Which popular 1990s brand had a kangaroo logo?

3. What was the preferred strap styling for dungarees in the 1990s?

4. Which make of work boot was popularized by 1990s hip-hop artists?

5 Which style of jean was created by tumbling the denim in bleach?

6 Which brand of slightly frog-eyed sports sunglasses were a big hit during the decade?

7 Which 1990s fashion commercial featured belly buttons singing along to Diana Ross's "I'm Coming Out"?

8 JNCO jeans were associated with fans of which sport?

Answers: 1. The Chrome Dome **2.** Kangol **3.** One strap undone **4.** Timberland **5.** Acid wash **6.** Oakley **7.** Levi's Super Low Jeans **8.** Skateboarding (and rollerblading)

115

YOU KNOW YOU'RE A CHILD OF THE 1990s WHEN...

You aspired to own a mountain bike with **RockShox**.

The words **"squeeze it"** are synonymous with consuming highly sugared, highly colored juice drinks served in a squishy plastic bottle.

A **Doodle Bear** was basically just a toy you could repeatedly destroy without concern.

Everything was **"phat"** (that's with a "ph").

The Dream Team

The 1992 Barcelona Olympic games saw what was probably the greatest roster of talent in the history of US basketball, with the US team featuring greats such as Michael Jordan, Larry Bird, and Magic Johnson.

Ken Griffey Jr.

Baseball Hall of Fame inductee and 13-time All-Star Griffey was our baseball hero back in the 90s. During his heyday with the Seattle Mariners and Cincinnati Reds he scored 627 of his 630 career home runs, and we all wanted a pair of Nike Air Griffey Max sneakers.

THE COMEBACK

In January 1993, the Buffalo Bills overcame a 32-point deficit to beat the Houston Oilers at New York's Rich Stadium. The Oilers were in the lead and the game had gone into overtime when Steve Christie kicked a 32-yard field goal, winning the game for the Bills in the greatest comeback in NFL history—a sporting moment referred to by many as simply "the comeback."

YOU KNOW YOU'RE A CHILD OF THE 1990s WHEN...

The immortal words
"We were on a break!"
still echoin your mind.

You thought that **French Bread Pizzas** were one of the best microwave foods ever invented.

You ate unholy amounts of **cereal** just to get more tiny plastic **prizes**... pencil toppers, spoon toppers, anything!

You were captivated by the idea of **an underground rave** (but had no clue how to find or get to one).

QUIZ

ONLY A CHILD OF THE 1990s WILL KNOW...

1. The exclamation "As if!" was popularized by which classic 1990s movie?

2. "Diss" was an abbreviation of what word?

3. "Dumb babies" was the go-to response of which *Rugrats* character?

4. Which Tom Hanks movie line was used to annoy joggers and people running to catch a train?

5 If someone isn't that impressive, they are not "all that and a bag of..." what?

6 Which cartoon duo coined the delightful term "fart-knocker"?

7 "Fo shizzle my nizzle" was popularized by which American rapper?

8 The "double loser" hand gesture could combine to create the sign for which other flippant phrase?

YOU KNOW YOU'RE A CHILD OF THE 1990s WHEN...

Your dream house is one entirely furnished with **inflatable** chairs.

Your parents used to have to physically pry you out of the **Discovery Zone**.

You had to go to the **DOS** part of your computer to launch **video games**.

You owned at least 30 different **scented gel pens**.

DO YOU REMEMBER...

Goosebumps books

They weren't kidding around when they said you were in for a scare. Never mind all the horror movies and violent video games your parents were trying to protect you from—the real nightmares were contained in these books.

Sweet Valley High

Oh those twins, just living normal lives as stunningly beautiful, wealthy teens surrounded by their similarly beautiful and wealthy friends. We couldn't get enough of all the low-stakes drama, make-ups, and break-ups that took place at *Sweet Valley High*.

Anne Fine

If Anne Fine had just written *Madame Doubtfire* then she would have been our childhood hero. But no, she whacked out winners like nobody's business: *Flour Babies*, *The Diary of a Killer Cat*, *Charm School*. We might as well have just had a shelf dedicated to her.

The Stinky Cheese Man

This postmodern fairy tale anthology parodied all the classics you'd come to know and love, featuring star characters including the Little Red Hen who never stopped complaining, Chicken Licken, who is crushed by the table of contents, and the Really Ugly Duckling that grew up to be a Really Ugly Duck.

Amelia's Notebooks

This series by Marissa Moss, filled with Amelia's thoughts, memories, and quirky doodles, helped us to navigate many of the common problems of being a kid, from how to make friends at school to how to deal with siblings, and how to survive a long car ride.

Wayside School series

Featuring evil teachers and students who all have something unusual about them, Louis Sachar's series set in a mysterious classroom on the 30th floor made you realize that maybe your own school wasn't so bad after all.

If you're interested in finding out more
about our books, find us on Facebook at
Summersdale Publishers and follow us on
Twitter at @Summersdale.

www.summersdale.com

IMAGE CREDITS

Sneakers – pp.5, 9, 13, 17, 21, 25, 29, 33, 37, 41, 45, 49, 53, 57, 61,
65, 69, 73, 77, 81, 85, 89, 93, 97, 101, 105, 109, 113, 117, 121, 125 ©
HintHunter/Shutterstock.com; water gun – pp.5, 9, 13, 17, 21, 25, 29,
33, 37, 41, 45, 49, 53, 57, 61, 65, 69, 73, 77, 81, 85, 89, 93, 97, 101,
105, 109, 113, 117, 121, 125 © Asya Alexandrova/Shutterstock.com;
Game Boy – pp.7, 128 © Rita Kovács; row of media icons © pp.11,19,
27, 35, 43, 51, 59, 67, 75, 83, 91, 99, 107, 115, 123 © SmileStudio/
Shutterstock.com; Bel-air – p.23 © Smith Sights/Shutterstock.
com; jelly sandals – p.39 © Rita Kovács; hairstyle – p.55 © Julie
Goldsmith; 'Not!' – p.71 © Rita Kovács; phone – p.79 © Rita Kovács;
'Nachos rule!!!' – p.95 © Julie Goldsmith; baby bottle pop – p.103
© Rita Kovács; Football – p.119 © Tetreb88/Shutterstock.com